# Revelations of a Secret Poet

By: Damion X

ISBN: 978-1-387-76848-6

# DEDICATION

*This book is dedicated to Rosa B. Williams (Grammy), Dr. Patricia Rouse and my entire family both present and transitioned. I'll run the remainder of the race for us until it's my time to rest.*

# ACKNOWLEDGMENTS

All praises to the Most High within for the gift of poetically articulating my emotions in order to navigate the world around me. I want to thank everyone who has ever supported me along my journey. To all who saw the light in me before I could see it for myself. Whether you knew it or not, you helped nurture me with affirmations of confirmations and you are a part of why I even chose to put my work out into the world. To my daughter Aa'Leiah, your smiles, laughter and existence fills my heart like no other substance in the universe, I love you beyond measure.

# CONTENTS

# The Evol

# of

# Love

# *Medusa*

I must be in love with the pain
that's the only way to explain
why I still love you,

Like a lucky shirt I wear the hurt
you gave me, and I can't seem to
find the strength to take it off

I hate the weakness I feel for you
cause you were once a stronghold
for me

Now you only have a stronghold over me
and you take advantage of how
I once thought we were meant to be

Any fool with eyes can see just how dangerously
quick and deep I had fallen, for you,
of course except for me

Medusa has done less damage in her time
than you've managed to do to the heart
of this man

I developed trust issues since you left me all alone,
my heart hasn't been the same since
you turned it into stone

I looked deep into your eyes and believed
all the lies that rolled off your tongue,
held under the spell of every line like the lyrics
to our favorite song

When you touched me, it took away all the pain
I kept inside, but you replaced it
with misery now that you're no longer
by my side

How could you just love me
when I'm down
then up and leave without so much as a sound

You cut me with your abrasiveness
even after we opened up,
you never really opened up with the intent
of healing, still hiding,
forever concealing never revealing

You held on to your past
and passed on your hurt to me,
the silence caused separation about
the same size of the sea

I didn't know loving you came
with such an insurmountable
emotional fee,

But I bought in to the point
of no return and got no you
in return
I guess it's just my turn to learn,

Like all fools who have
fallen for Medusa…

# *Devil in the Dashiki*

Excuse me sir,
have you seen the devil in the dashiki?
I must warn you she'll melt your heart
and turn it into liquid

She's ten times hotter than the
surface of the sun, if you dare
look her in the eyes you
are as good as done

Don't be fooled by the innocence of her face
or fall for that devilish smile

She's no good, although it's all good
in the beginning, in the end
she'll have you feeling all bad

She'll lure you in with those distinguishing
features of beauty

She can spit fire like venom
with her tongue,
and make you forget about the pain
of the burn

She'll get into your veins and course through
your body and make you
yearn for her

You'll sell all your possessions
to possess her,
but, in reality, she'll really possess you

Beware of the sweet nectar
that drips from betwixt her lips,
one sip and you'll slip
into paralysis unable to walk away,

If you stay with her to long
she'll eventually do you wrong
and know just what to say to make
everything alright,

All night you'll stay up
waiting for her
even though she's long gone,
she's moved on to who or where
nobody knows but her,

Excuse me sir,
have you seen the devil in the dashiki?

# *Murder She Wrote 1*

Put your ear to my chest
and feel the cold echoing absence
of a heart that use to beat for you

A tragic casualty
it now ceases to work
since you ripped it in two

My love, my Leo, my lioness
with the locs
you had my love on lock,
and just threw away the key
metaphorically you just did away with me

You showed no remorse
and without indication you chose
to change our course

Screaming for you to come back,
and my voice has gone hoarse

When it comes to the future
your name I no longer feel safe to mention,
have you not noticed
or ignored my desperate attempts
to get your attention?

Well past due is the time to apologize,
if ever I get the chance to see
those beautiful brown eyes,

I would not look for fear
that I would be hypnotized
and no longer recollect the pain
on the inside

It pains me more,
that my love
for you still deeply resides,
like fire and ice trying
to coexist side by side

You cut me deeper than
I've been cut before,
you've mortally wounded the inner
optimist that I once was at the core…

# *Murder She Wrote 2*

I'll never again be what I once was
the day after we met…

A fool falling in love,
cause the pain from the heartache
won't let me forget--
to never let someone in,
no not ever again,
will another like she have a chance at
hurting the real me,

You see,

In the beginning I was convinced you
were my karma
for my womanizing past,
but I told myself no retribution
would come from falling for you
this is the love that will last

Then bang!

My eyes filled with tears
at that moment cause
I knew I was hit,
helpless cause I could do nothing
to prevent
I just knew this was it

There was this pain that I never felt before,
it was a gun shot to my heart
and I collapse to the floor

D.O.A,
flatline…

The culprit left no evidence behind,
she left the scene after committing
the perfect love crime,

Now her face is posted
on the most wanted sign,
for committing
the most unwarranted heinous act
of all time…

The murder of my heart…

# *No Resuscitation*

I'm a strong man and there's a lot
that I can take,
but woman a life without you
is the point where I break,
and I'm breaking down right now
some how a sad clown
depicts my face
and no matter how hard I try
I can't erase this look off my face

I've been miserable since the day we lost touch,
I wrote you three times
expressing how I love you so much
and I can't get through this without
your loving support,
I appreciate every time you managed to
make it to court

I find it hard to smile these days
my heart is trapped in a surreal
feeling emotional daze,
if this love is true
I really need it to come through,
I really need to hear you say it,
say you love me too!

This void between us has put me in a hole
of distress, even if you don't
want me, I still love you no less

Every letter I get
and I see it's not from you,
drives my heart to collide at high speeds
of emotion splitting in two,

I'm at the point of desperation,
your love gave my love
reason for respiration,
so without it
I sign off,
no resuscitation…

# *Does Love Always Prevail?*

I'm sick of writing lovesick poems
waiting and wondering,
missing you and wishing you
would come see me or write me back,
it's been forever
and I'm suffering from a lack
of contact

My mind keeps playing games
I don't want to play,
drifting in and out
in between the state of sleep and awake

I so desperately just want to get away
to find a way to feel better,

yet I remain stuck,

My heart and mental do battle over you,
yes, you this is all over you
I long to be all over you
like we use to be

Even when I close my eyes it's you I see
and I can't stand to see the pictures of
you and me, because it hurts;
and I don't know why, but I question my heart
like why?

While I'm still in jail,

Is it true what they say,

Does love always prevail?

# *A Spell Apart*

Last time we talked
I didn't see that fire in your eyes
like I use to,
has the fight to maintain this love
gotten the best of you

I know I'm not there like I should be
and it's not fair cause you could be
living your life without the stress
of the mess
I'm in,

I'm fighting for my life
as well as
the love of my life
I'm struggling, and it feels like
my world is caving in
I feel like we're losing it, but I want
us to win
to stop the end
to what we started
where do I begin?

A future without you
woman,
that don't even sound right,
I hope I'm not outta your mind
even though I been outta your sight
I'll do whatever it takes to make it right
I lay awake on my bunk in the darkness of night
with my heart on repeat for you despite,
my predicament

Love and happiness mingle whenever
we're together,
let us dance our way through
this rain and stormy weather

Let us not ever forget our long prosperous
talks of forever,
remember how forever
never seemed long enough for us?

I know this is the hard part,
but I know in my heart this spell
won't be the cause that we're forever apart…

# *Messed Up pt. I*

Baby can't you see
I'm so messed up over you
I'm crying tears so intense
you can see them turning blue

My heart is aching
my whole world is shaken
since your love for me has been taken

I see you in my dreams
but you're a ghost in my reality
an emotional solar eclipse
got me stuck in the darkness of totality

Why is it now
you just refuse to come back to me?
this has quickly escalated
into a tragic catastrophe,
but we can fix this right?

This love felt so real,
now it's surrealistic and I can't tell what's unreal,
clarify to me exactly how you feel
exactly how time between us stood still,
exactly how my love you managed to steal
before you
I thought my heart was made of steel…

# *Messed up pt. II*

Love is all fun and games
until somebody gets seriously hurt

It can give birth to the death
of the part of you that was invincible,
conceive in your mind the most unthinkable,
make you a victim witness
to the most detestable,

Bring about questions
concerning the unquestionable

Love you're a beautiful villain in disguise
collaborating with the woman
of my dreams
orchestrating my demise,
my trust in you I never thought you'd compromise,
your honesty just turned out to be
an exquisite collage of lies

You sold me a fairytale beginning,
and wounded me deeply
with the horror story ending

So, to the next woman in my life,
I'll be a man and fess up,
my trust issues come from her and love
they're the explanation
as to why and how I became
so messed up…

# *True Love Thing*

I once believed in true love,
and it turned around and bite me in the rear,
oh dear,
how it hurt my heart so
cause she was so close to my heart

I believed every word she said
until her actions showed me otherwise
I can't believe I believed and bought into those
believable lies,
or maybe
they were true at one point in time,
but time away
poor communication and circumstances
changed all that

I now think I just need some time away
some time to be better acquainted with myself
it'll be some time
before my guard goes down and I open up
to someone else

I don't want to be selfish,
but I did my best to be selfless
and I see what that got me

A first-class ticket next to lonely on the train,
destination lonely Ville,
for her I would kill,
as a matter of fact I did,
the old player part of me was put to rest
I gave up the games and gave her the best
of me
resetting myself
preparing for matrimony

Unlearning all the dirty tricks of the trade
actually caring and not just caring
to get laid

This woman was an unprecedented
force of nature in my life,
I've done my fair share of wrong
but she motivated me to do right
now she's nowhere to be seen
vanished completely out of sight

Somehow my heart still wants to hold on
even if only by a string,
this must be the inglorious part
of this so-called True Love Thing…

# The Light that came from Darkness

# *I Get It*

I get it,

I know the feeling of pain
so heavy on your chest
your lungs feel like they're
about to collapse

You desperately try to collect air
while you recollect
the what, when, and where
it got so bad

Its' gotten to the point
you're willing to appoint
the hurt supreme,
king,
cause it rules with an iron fist

Without relent,
it's like life events
are hell bent
on taking you under
at night
I sit in the dark and wonder,

What's next?

Why me?

Why this?

Why is the end the only thing
I can't see,
okay is the only thing I can't be?

I get it,

I can relate,
the cold misery of mystery
in relation to fate,
existentialism
got me contemplating an early
expiration date,

I just need to escape,
so don't judge my fascination
with isolation
before you take into
consideration
my struggles with communication,

I've been in constant miscommunication
with elation
in disconnect with the highest vibration
and on occasion
I'm not myself due to frustration
lashing out
cause I'm in doubt about
what this is all about

Echoes of a time when life made sense
or at least I was ignorant with bliss
aiming for that youthful freedom
is a target I always miss,

I get it,

I've reached my peak
of being strong
this is why I'm feeling so weak
and I'm tired of being silent
I've had enough of being meek
if relief doesn't come soon
I fear I'll see defeat,

Whatever that means,

if you look in my eyes
exhaustion can clearly be seen,
my face is likened to an emotional
movie scene
and if it moves you
it's cause I feel you,
and I just want to tell you,

I get it…

# *Why I Gotta Get Out*

This is why I gotta get out,
cause my free spirit is unfamiliar
with the constraints of this
concrete box,

Despite my strength my wings
can't expand and bend
these steel bars
reinforced by fake justice
my dreams are too big
for this small building,

I can't get a grasp on this reality
it doesn't make sense
to my soul to be in so much pain,
but I keep being told the blessing
is worth the wait so,

This is why I gotta get out,

Foreign are my beliefs to my circumstances
and the odds are stacked
against me but I'll take my chances
in this fight
to the spiritual death,
my light they seek to put out
but I'll show them what Ms. Stine son
is about,

This is why I gotta get out,

This is an ocean of sorrow
and I keep kicking
cause I don't want to drown
and miss my tomorrow,
if I could just borrow and extend
your attention span
to hear the plight of this young man,
maybe just maybe,
I could trigger a chain reaction
to bring about some satisfaction
to a 'satisfaction-less' system

This is why I gotta get out,

Incomprehensible
unless you been through it,
I've been pushed to the brink
and I was just about to lose it,
until a voice told me
don't you dare do it
hang on you're almost there
I know the process seems unfair,
but you got one hell of a
story to share

This is why I gotta get out…

# *What They Won't Do*

Come here,
let me elevate you with education
inspire you with knowledge
not previously known,
but needed
in order to knock down
the walls of ignorance,

You leave me in despair
knowing your completely unaware
of the affects
of your egregious dialect,
every time you open your mouth
you open up a vein,
spewing the blood of the millions
that were slain,

Disrespecting the thousands that marched
for our treatment to be the same,
as everyone else,
and you should know better than anyone else
exactly what we went through
and I know you
learn the truth in school,
but in this day and age
you must make an effort to remain a fool

Not trying to learn,
not trying to improve,
do you not know where?
or do you just not care
to put the time into
looking up
the information
that will lead to
a gradual transformation
in the way you look at the world
and conduct yourself

A mind is a terrible thing to waste,
but keep in mind
that the time you have
is not time to waste
cultivate your being
expand your horizon past the stereotype
they say you are,

Challenge yourself to surpass
what you consider to be too far

You have to see yourself
doing it before it gets done,

Doing what no one else will isn't always fun,
but remember
You're just doing what they won't do…

# *Lifeline*

Assuredly there is one thing
that I know,
after the rain fall on the Serengeti
the rivers fill
and the green grass begins to grow

I have more to offer
than you may think
it doesn't take more than
a moment
to stop and think

Although when you're down,
depressed or irate
it's hard to hear when told
to contemplate,
when emotions are strong
and feelings escalate
consider the outcome before
it's too late,

A brash and rash decision
you need not make,
this could lead to an irrevocable mistake

This is something you should not
take for granted
cause for every action there's a reaction,
for every cause there is an effect
that could affect you for a lifetime

So for the sake of your life,
please,
use a lifeline…

# *Recalcitrant*

I mean this when I say
I can't help
but to be a revolutionary,

It's in my blood linked to my melanin
I'll give my sweat and tears
for the cause of causing
change for my people

I can't stand the pain I see in the eyes
of my people,
for to long we've been treated
to the equivalent of unequal

We've been lied to, yes, they've even
tried to erase our history
from the face of the earth,
but check the origins of the place
of the oldest remains ever found
on earth

Back to the land of the great mother
you must go,
read more books written by us
and the truth you'll begin to know

Sift through the whitewashed fictious facts
about aboriginal history
read between the white lies
and unravel the paradoxical mystery

My heroes consist of the FBI's
black most wanted list,
they taught me to love the skin I'm in
and not shuck n' jive and grin
or fear in the presence of
white men

My words are like the elixir
you could get from a
speak-easy,
if you're not an advocate
of black love it'll make
your heart, soul, and stomach
a little queasy

Open, read, and comprehend
start a conversation on
self-love
and watch how we start to win

It's a silent war for our soul
and I rebel against control
I'm a recalcitrant
man of old
and I don't fit the stereotypical mold…

# *I AM who I AM*

I am who I am,
and my thoughts are like
a tumultuous wave
on the sea during a storm,
outside of the box not of the norm
meant to cause no harm
with a subtle charm,

My words flow like water
disturbing the peace of disorder,
an oxymoronic way of thinking
like the joker,
but I'm not crazy

I'm a soulful misfit,
who represents the soul
of the discontented,
my soul is on a mission
and to this earth I've been sent

From the Most High
I've been given consent
to speak my truth
and shall not tell a lie,
I'm a rebel so I do not comply
or rely on your attempt
to define me

I define myself,
I look in the mirror for acceptance
and not to anyone else,
like a gold tooth
I shine and stand out
desperately seeking attention
is not what I'm about
I desperately seek your attention
to try and get you out
of the matrix you've been trapped in

Every misconception you been
believing has been subtracting
from your
fullest potential
preventing you from becoming
the quintessential, Neo,
the One,

Who can save You is You,
but you have to whole heartedly
really want too,
get out of your current paradigm
and shift your mode
to critical thinking,

Inception,
a spinning top type of explanation,
there are some that won't get it,
but it you with it
I'm with it,
my right to live free will not be
forfeited
what my ancestors,
not now
nor will I ever forget it

I’ve been pitted
against the system, in route
to completing a daunting task,
I’m not the first
and I won’t be the last,
to
pave a liberated way to the future,
due to my past,
Life is a marathon
and I can’t burn myself out
trying to move to fast

Pass me the torch
cause I’m ignited with change,
to change
things with anyone that will listen
my goal is to be a
revolutionary premonition
a living breathing superstition
a cure for any pre-existing condition,
those who are well have no
need for a physician,
in my world
I see the world with optimism
and philosophical artistic vision

It's a radical decision,
to live your life
for something bigger than self,
to be engrossed
with the welfare of people, the planet
or a purpose
bigger than gaining personal wealth,
to know your actions
affect those around you
letting empathetic compassion
be the anchor that grounds you
I saw true love who
looked me in the face
and said
finally I found you

Now I'm not letting you go,
planting spiritual
seeds of self-respect,
knowledge of self,
kindness, peace, and patience
cultivating with love
to assure they grow,
all the while
letting everyone know,
I AM
who I AM…

*The End…*

"In the midst of turmoil, confusion, hurt and depravity find the inner light that makes enough noise to guide you to salvation" – Damion X.

www.ingramcontent.com/pod-product-compliance
Ingram Content Group UK Ltd.
Pitfield, Milton Keynes, MK11 3LW, UK
UKHW041835200726
13854UKWH00003BA/1155